DID SOMEONE SAY CAKE?

A Dozen Quilts from 10" Layer Cake Squares

Compiled by **Lissa Alexander**

Martingale
Create with Confidence

Moda Bake Shop
Did Someone Say *Cake*?
A Dozen Quilts from 10" Layer Cake Squares
© 2022 by Martingale & Company®

Martingale®
18939 120th Ave NE, Suite 101
Bothell, WA 98011-9511 USA
ShopMartingale.com

Printed in Hong Kong
27 26 25 24 23 22   8 7 6 5 4 3 2 1

Library of Congress Cataloging-in-Publication Data is available upon request.

ISBN: 978-1-68356-170-5

MISSION STATEMENT

We empower makers who use fabric and yarn to make life more enjoyable.

CREDITS

PUBLISHER AND CHIEF VISIONARY OFFICER
Jennifer Erbe Keltner

CONTENT DIRECTOR
Karen Costello Soltys

DESIGN MANAGER
Adrienne Smitke

TECHNICAL EDITOR
Nancy Mahoney

PRODUCTION MANAGER
Regina Girard

COPY EDITOR
Melissa Bryan

PHOTOGRAPHER
Brent Kane

ILLUSTRATOR
Sandy Loi

  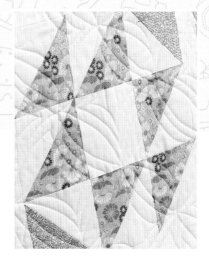

Contents

INTRODUCTION

Who doesn't love cake? Whether it's the kind you eat or the colorful fabric variety, we're all in. And you will be too! Especially when the Moda Bake Shop chefs show you how easy it is to turn a stack of coordinated precut 10" Layer Cake squares into a beautiful quilt you can enjoy for years to come.

Each pattern starts with the same basic ingredients—a Moda Fabrics Layer Cake and yardage of a background fabric—but the quilts can turn out surprisingly different, depending on which fabrics you start with. From the secondary pattern that emerges in Amanda Wilbert's Spice Cake bed quilt (page 7) to the undulating waves of Audrey Mann and Diane Brinton's Beaded Bracelets design (page 11) to Lauren Terry's striking two-color Mountaintop lap quilt (page 57), you'll be amazed at just how different and tempting each Layer Cake quilt pattern is.

So, whether you raid your pantry, er, fabric stash for the Layer Cakes you have on hand or you shop for a few new favorites based on the colors and patterns showcased in this book, you're bound to find the perfect Layer Cake recipe to suit your taste. In fact, this is one quilt recipe book you'll turn to again and again!

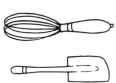

SPICE CAKE

FROM THE KITCHEN OF: *amanda wilbert*

The half-square triangle is one of the most versatile shapes in patchwork. While playing around with some triangles, Amanda discovered that with careful fabric placement and a few strategically positioned sashing squares she could add a fun secondary pattern to her quilt design.

FINISHED QUILT: 80" × 80" FINISHED BLOCKS: 12" × 12"

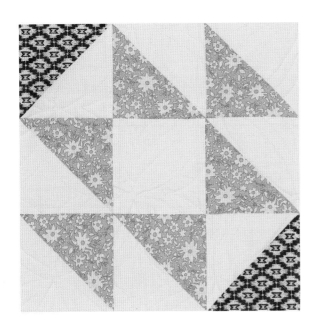

MATERIALS

Yardage is based on 42"-wide fabric. A Moda Fabrics Layer Cake contains 42 squares, 10" × 10". Amanda used Cider by BasicGrey for Moda Fabrics.

- 36 squares, 10" × 10", of assorted dark prints for blocks
- 4¾ yards of white solid for blocks and sashing
- ⅞ yard of navy print for sashing squares and binding
- 7⅓ yards of fabric for backing
- 88" × 88" piece of batting

CUTTING

All measurements include ¼" seam allowances.

From *each* of the dark print squares, cut:
4 squares, 5" × 5" (144 total)

From the white solid, cut:
18 strips, 5" × 42"; crosscut into 144 squares, 5" × 5"
5 strips, 4½" × 42"; crosscut into 36 squares, 4½" × 4½"
3 strips, 12½" × 42"; crosscut into 60 strips, 2" × 12½"
1 strip, 2" × 42"; crosscut into 12 squares, 2" × 2"

From the navy print, cut:
9 strips, 2½" × 42"
1 strip, 2" × 42"; crosscut into 13 squares, 2" × 2"

plan ahead

As you cut the dark 10" squares into smaller squares, set aside one 5" square from each print. When choosing fabrics for each block, pick an accent print from these separate squares. Keeping the accent squares separate from the others will ensure that a particular print is not used as an accent square more than once. If you do use an accent print more than once, you won't have enough matching squares to make all of the blocks.

MAKING THE BLOCKS

For each block, choose three matching dark 5"
squares and one dark 5" square of a different print
to be the accent print. Repeat to make 36 stacks
of dark squares. Press seam allowances in the
directions indicated by the arrows.

1 Select one stack of dark squares and four
white 5" squares. Draw a diagonal line from
corner to corner on the wrong side of the white
squares. Layer a marked square on a dark square,
right sides together. Sew ¼" from both sides of the
drawn line. Cut the unit apart on the marked line to

make two half-square-triangle units. Trim the units to 4½" square, including seam allowances. Make eight half-square-triangle units.

4½"

4½"

Make 8 units.

2 Lay out the half-square-triangle units from step 1 and one white 4½" square in three rows, noting the orientation of the units. Sew the units and square into rows. Join the rows to make a block measuring 12½" square, including seam allowances. Repeat the steps to make 36 blocks.

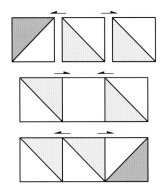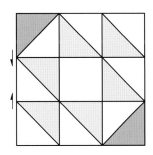

Make 36 blocks,
12½" × 12½".

ASSEMBLING THE QUILT TOP

1 Join six blocks and five white 2" × 12½" strips, rotating the blocks according to the diagram to make block row A. Make three rows measuring 12½" × 80", including seam allowances. Repeat to make three B block rows, making sure to reverse the orientation of the blocks.

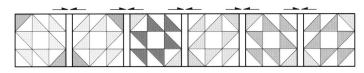

Make 3 A rows, 12½" × 80".

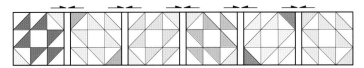

Make 3 B rows, 12½" × 80".

2 Join six white 2" × 12½" strips, three navy squares, and two white 2" squares to make sashing row C. Make three rows. Join six white strips, two navy squares, and three white 2" squares to make sashing row D. Make two rows. The sashing rows should measure 2" × 80", including seam allowances.

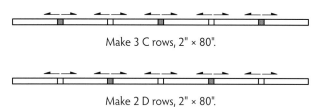

Make 3 C rows, 2" × 80".

Make 2 D rows, 2" × 80".

3 Join the block rows and sashing rows in alternating positions as shown in the quilt assembly diagram below. The quilt top should measure 80" square.

FINISHING THE QUILT

For more details on any finishing steps, visit ShopMartingale.com/HowtoQuilt for free downloadable information.

1 Layer the quilt top with batting and backing; baste the layers together.

2 Quilt by hand or machine. Amanda's quilt is machine quilted with a double pumpkin-seed design.

3 Use the navy 2½"-wide strips to make double-fold binding. Attach the binding to the quilt.

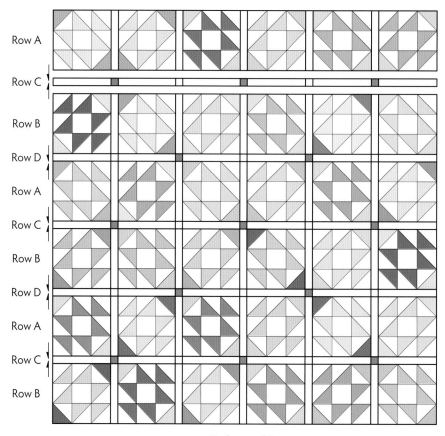

Quilt assembly

BEADED BRACELETS

FROM THE KITCHEN OF: *audrey mann & diane brinton*

Try your hand at curved piecing with gentle curves, sewn one block at a time. They may not be as quick to make as strip-pieced blocks, but the result is worth it. The overall effect is one of gentle waves rippling up and down throughout the quilt top.

FINISHED QUILT: 51½" × 67"   FINISHED BLOCKS: 8½" × 9½"

MATERIALS

Yardage is based on 42"-wide fabric. A Moda Fabrics Layer Cake contains 42 squares, 10" × 10". Audrey and Diane used Ma Morris Studio from the V&A Archives by Minick and Simpson for Moda Fabrics.

- 42 squares, 10" × 10", of assorted prints for blocks
- ⅝ yard of black solid for binding
- 3¼ yards of fabric for backing
- 58" × 73" piece of batting
- Template plastic

CUTTING

Before you begin cutting, trace patterns A and B on pages 16 and 17 onto template plastic and cut them out. Use the templates to cut the A and B pieces from the print 10" squares, referring to the cutting diagram below as needed. All measurements include ¼" seam allowances.

From *each* of the assorted print squares, cut:
1 of A (42 total)
2 of B (84 total)

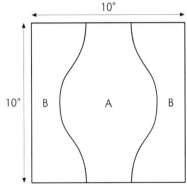

Cutting for squares

From the black solid, cut:
7 strips, 2½" × 42"

MAKING THE BLOCKS

Press seam allowances in the directions indicated by the arrows.

1 Select two matching B pieces and one contrasting A piece. Fold each piece in half and finger-press to mark the midpoints. Place a B piece on top of the A piece, right sides together, matching the center fold; pin in place. Align and pin the pieces at each end.

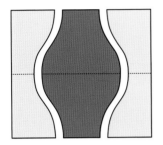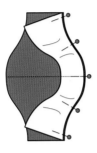

2 With the edges aligned, sew along the curved edge, easing or gently stretching both fabrics as needed while you sew. In the same way, pin and sew the second B piece to the opposite side to make a block. Make 42 blocks measuring 9" × 10", including seam allowances.

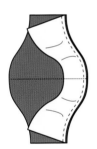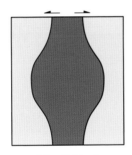

Make 42 blocks,
9" × 10".

divide and conquer

If you're experienced at piecing curves, pinning the two ends and at the midpoint may suffice. But if you're not quite comfortable with curves yet, divide the space between one end and the midpoint, and pin halfway in between. Then divide each of the resulting sections in half again and pin. Sew slowly from one pin to the next and you'll be a curve expert before you know it!

ASSEMBLING THE QUILT TOP

Lay out the blocks in seven rows of six blocks each as shown in the quilt assembly diagram below. Sew the blocks into rows. Join the rows to complete the quilt top, which should measure 51½" × 67".

FINISHING THE QUILT

For more details on any finishing steps, visit ShopMartingale.com/HowtoQuilt for free downloadable information.

1 Layer the quilt top with batting and backing; baste the layers together.

2 Quilt by hand or machine. Audrey and Diane's quilt is machine quilted with a flower bouquet motif in each of the A pieces and a large spiral in each of the B pieces.

3 Use the black 2½"-wide strips to make double-fold binding. Attach the binding to the quilt.

Quilt assembly

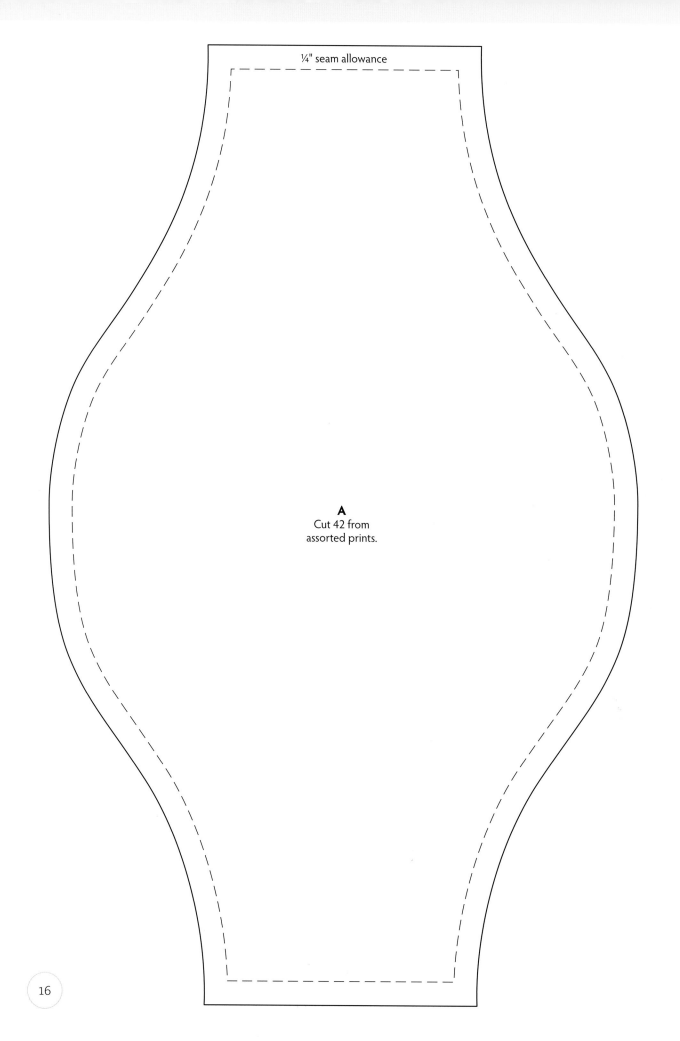

¼" seam allowance

A
Cut 42 from
assorted prints.

¼" seam allowance

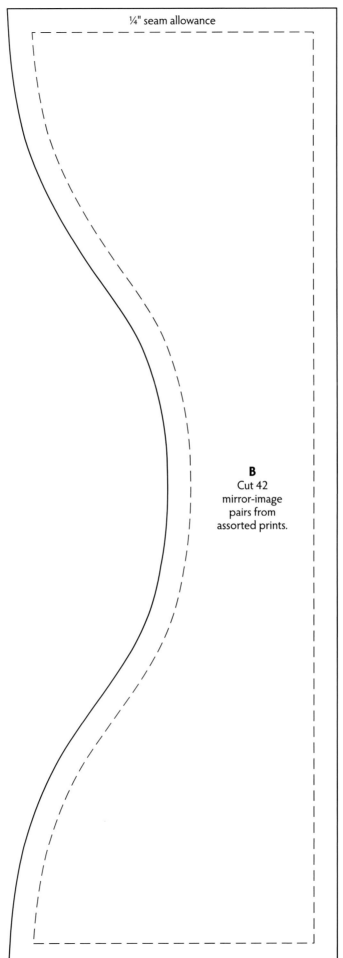

¼" seam allowance

B
Cut 42
mirror-image
pairs from
assorted prints.

¼" seam allowance

JEWELED DIAMONDS

FROM THE KITCHEN OF: *michele kuhns*

Stitch your own string of jewel-toned diamonds in this beautiful batik quilt. Making this project even more special is that you'll have enough squares in your Layer Cake to make not only the quilt, but also the table runner and a patchwork pillow! These diamonds are sure to please.

FINISHED QUILT: 72½" × 80½"   **FINISHED BLOCKS: 8" × 8"**

MATERIALS

Yardage is based on 42"-wide fabric. A Moda Fabrics Layer Cake contains 42 squares, 10" × 10". Michele used Malibu Batiks and Bella Solids by Moda Fabrics.

- 33 squares, 10" × 10", of assorted dark batiks for blocks
- 4¼ yards of white solid *OR* 2 Layer Cakes in white solid for blocks
- ⅝ yard of aqua print for binding
- 6¾ yards of fabric for backing
- 81" × 89" piece of batting

CUTTING

All measurements include ¼" seam allowances.

From *each* of the dark batik squares, cut:
4 squares, 5" × 5" (132 total)

From the white solid, cut:
17 strips, 5" × 42"; crosscut into 132 squares, 5" × 5"
6 strips, 8½" x 42"; crosscut into 24 squares, 8½" x 8½" (Note: If using white Layer Cakes, cut 33 of the squares into quarters to yield 132 squares, 5" x 5". Trim 24 Layer Cake squares to 8½" x 8½".)

From the aqua print, cut:
8 strips, 2½" × 42"

MAKING THE BLOCKS

Press all seam allowances open as indicated by the arrows.

1 Draw a diagonal line from corner to corner on the wrong side of the white 5" squares. Layer a marked square on a dark 5" square, right sides together. Sew ¼" from both sides of the drawn line. Cut the unit apart on the marked line to make two half-square-triangle units. Trim the units to measure 4½" square, including seam allowances. Make 264 units.

Make 264 units.

2 Lay out four assorted half-square-triangle units in two rows, rotating the units to form a diamond shape. Sew the units into rows. Join the rows to make a Diamond block measuring 8½" square, including seam allowances. Make 66 blocks.

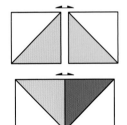 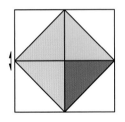

Make 66 Diamond blocks,
8½" × 8½".

keep it together

Michele prefers to press all of the seam allowances open to reduce bulk. To ensure that the seams don't pop open, she recommends starting and ending every seam with a backstitch.

ASSEMBLING THE QUILT TOP

Referring to the quilt assembly diagram below, lay out the Diamond and Four Patch blocks and the white 8½" squares in 10 rows of nine blocks each as shown in the quilt assembly diagram below. Sew the blocks into rows. Join the rows to complete the quilt top, which should measure 72½" × 80½".

FINISHING THE QUILT

For more details on any finishing steps, visit ShopMartingale.com/HowtoQuilt for free downloadable information.

1 Layer the quilt top with batting and backing; baste the layers together.

2 Quilt by hand or machine. Michele's quilt is machine quilted with an allover scroll design.

3 Use the aqua 2½"-wide strips to make double-fold binding and then attach the binding to the quilt.

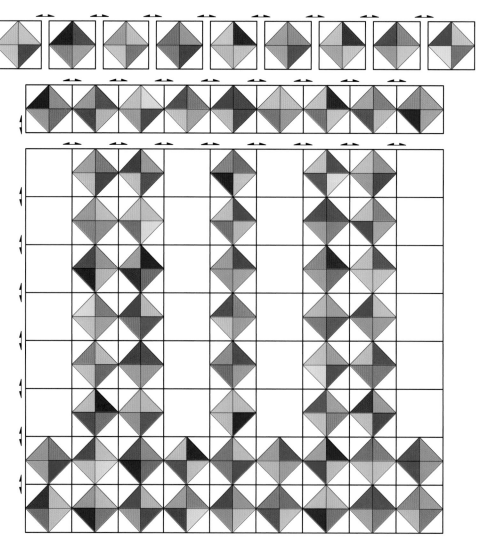

Quilt assembly

Don't Waste Your Cake

To make a 44½" × 10½" table runner, you'll need five pieced blocks,
¼ yard of white solid for the border, and ¼ yard of aqua print for binding.
To make a 16½" square pillow, you'll need four pieced blocks, ½ yard of
fabric for the pillow back, and ¼ yard of aqua print for binding.

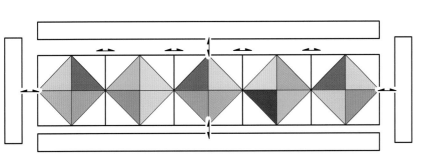

Table runner assembly

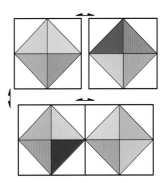

Pillow-top assembly

GARDEN GATE

FROM THE KITCHEN OF: *jen daly*

You don't have to have a green thumb to enjoy a beautiful cottage garden, as long as you have a sewing machine! Stitch a generous-sized lap quilt that works just as well at the foot of a bed as it does on your couch, and you'll be basking in the beauty of big luscious blooms all year round.

FINISHED QUILT: 56½" × 68½" FINISHED BLOCKS: 10½" × 10½"

MATERIALS

Yardage is based on 42"-wide fabric. A Moda Fabrics Layer Cake contains 42 squares, 10" × 10". Jen used Strawberries and Rhubarb by Fig Tree Quilts for Moda Fabrics.

- 40 squares, 10" × 10", of assorted prints for blocks, sashing squares, and pieced outer border
- 2⅝ yards of cream print for blocks, sashing, and inner border

- ⅝ yard of coral print for binding
- 3½ yards of fabric for backing
- 63" × 75" piece of batting

CUTTING

Refer to the cutting diagrams below and on page 26 as needed to cut the 10" squares. All measurements include ¼" seam allowances.

From *each* of 10 assorted print squares, cut:
5 squares, 2" × 2" (50 total)
3 squares, 2½" × 2½" (30 total)
4 squares, 3½" × 3½" (40 total)

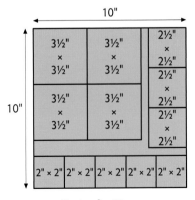

Cutting for 10 squares

Continued on page 26

Continued from page 25

From *each* of 10 assorted print squares, cut:

7 squares, 2½" × 2½" (70 total; 8 are extra)

4 squares, 3½" × 3½" (40 total)

```
                    10"
        ┌──────────┬──────────┬─────────┐
        │  3½"     │   3½"    │  2½"    │
        │   ×      │    ×     │   ×     │
        │  3½"     │   3½"    │  2½"    │
        │          │          ├─────────┤
        │          │          │  2½"    │
        │          │          │   ×     │
 10"    │  3½"     │   3½"    │  2½"    │
        │   ×      │    ×     ├─────────┤
        │  3½"     │   3½"    │  2½"    │
        │          │          │   ×     │
        │          │          │  2½"    │
        ├─────┬────┼─────┬────┼─────────┤
        │ 2½" │2½" │ 2½" │    │  2½"    │
        │  ×  │ ×  │  ×  │    │   ×     │
        │ 2½" │2½" │ 2½" │    │  2½"    │
        └─────┴────┴─────┴────┴─────────┘
```
Cutting for 10 squares

From *each* of 10 assorted print squares, cut:

4 pieces, 3½" × 5" (40 total)

5 squares, 2" × 2" (50 total)

From *each* of 10 assorted print squares, cut:

4 pieces, 3½" × 5" (40 total)

4 squares, 2½" × 2½" (40 total)

From the cream print, cut:

14 strips, 2½" × 42"; crosscut *11 of the strips*
    into 31 strips, 2½" × 11"

3 strips, 2¼" × 42"

20 strips, 2" × 42"; crosscut into 400 squares,
    2" × 2"

From the coral print, cut:

7 strips, 2½" × 42"

MAKING THE BLOCKS

Press seam allowances in the directions indicated
by the arrows.

1 Draw a diagonal line from corner to corner
on the wrong side of 320 cream 2" squares.

2 Place a marked cream square on one corner
of a print 3½" square, right sides together.
Sew on the marked line. Trim the excess corner
fabric ¼" from the stitched line. Place a marked
cream square on the opposite corner of the print
square. Sew and trim as before to make a leaf unit
measuring 3½" square, including seam allowances.
Make 80 units.

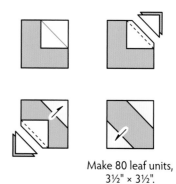

Make 80 leaf units,
3½" × 3½".

3 Place marked cream squares on adjacent
corners of a print 3½" × 5" piece, right sides
together. Sew on the marked lines. Trim the excess
corner fabric ¼" from the stitched lines. Make 80
petal units measuring 3½" × 5", including seam
allowances.

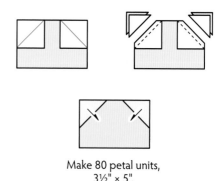

Make 80 petal units,
3½" × 5".

4 Lay out five matching print 2" squares and
four cream 2" squares in three rows. Sew
the squares into rows. Join the rows to make a
nine-patch unit measuring 5" square, including
seam allowances. Make 20 units.

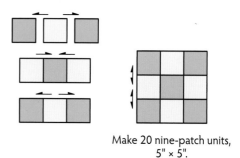

Make 20 nine-patch units,
5" × 5".

5 Lay out four matching leaf units, four matching petal units, and one nine-patch unit in three rows. Sew the units into rows. Join the rows to make a block measuring 11" square, including seam allowances. Make 20 blocks.

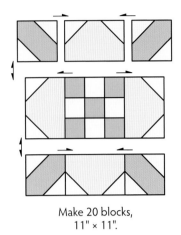

Make 20 blocks,
11" × 11".

ASSEMBLING THE QUILT-TOP CENTER

1 Join four blocks and three cream 2½" × 11" strips to make a block row. Make five rows measuring 11" × 48½", including seam allowances.

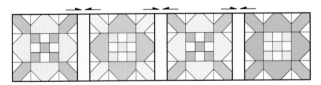

Make 5 block rows,
11" × 48½".

2 Join four cream 2½" × 11" strips and three print 2½" squares to make a sashing row. Make four rows measuring 2½" × 48½", including seam allowances.

Make 4 sashing rows,
2½" × 48½".

3 Join the block rows and sashing rows in alternating positions as shown in the quilt assembly diagram on page 29. The quilt-top center should measure 48½" × 61", including seam allowances.

ADDING THE BORDERS

1 Join the remaining cream 2½"-wide strips end to end. From the pieced strip, cut two 61"-long strips. Sew the strips to opposite sides of the quilt center.

2 Join the cream 2¼"-wide strips end to end. From the pieced strip, cut two 52½"-long strips. Sew the strips to the top and bottom edges of the quilt top. The quilt top should measure 52½" × 64½", including seam allowances.

3 Join 32 print 2½" squares to make a side border measuring 2½" × 64½", including seam allowances. Make two. Join 28 print 2½" squares to make a top border measuring 2½" × 56½", including seam allowances. Repeat to make the bottom border.

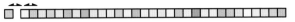

Make 2 side borders, 2½" × 64½".

Make 2 top/bottom borders, 2½" × 56½".

4 Sew the 64½"-long borders to opposite sides of the quilt top. Sew the 56½"-long borders to the top and bottom edges. The quilt top should measure 56½" × 68½".

FINISHING THE QUILT

For more details on any finishing steps, visit ShopMartingale.com/HowtoQuilt for free downloadable information.

1 Layer the quilt top with batting and backing; baste the layers together.

2 Quilt by hand or machine. Jen's quilt is machine quilted with an allover design of circles and loops.

3 Use the coral 2½"-wide strips to make double-fold binding. Attach the binding to the quilt.

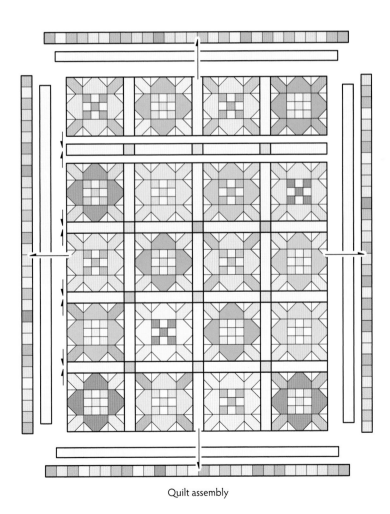

Quilt assembly

CARTWHEELS AND ROUNDOFFS

FROM THE KITCHEN OF: *lisa jo girodat*

Gymnastics has been popular in Lisa Jo's family for generations; she loves seeing the joy on a child's face after landing a perfect cartwheel or roundoff for the first time. Even if your tumbling days are long gone, you're sure to fall head over heels for Lisa Jo's unique Tumbling Pinwheels block.

FINISHED QUILT: 63½" × 81½" FINISHED BLOCKS: 16" × 16"

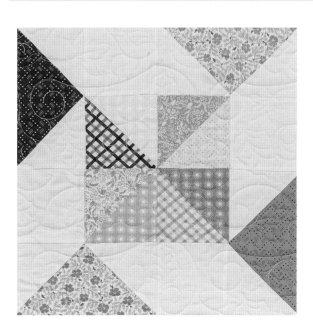

MATERIALS

Yardage is based on 42"-wide fabric. A Moda Fabrics Layer Cake contains 42 squares, 10" × 10". See "Change It Up" below. Lisa Jo used Flowers for Freya by Linzee McCray for Moda Fabrics.

- 38 squares, 10" × 10", of assorted dark prints for blocks and sashing squares

- 3¾ yards of white solid for blocks and sashing

- ⅓ yard of teal solid for inner border

- ¾ yard of teal floral for outer border

- ⅝ yard of navy print for binding

- 5 yards of fabric for backing

- 72" × 90" piece of batting

change it up

Lisa Jo made four sets of three identical blocks for her quilt. If you want to do the same, you'll need two matching Layer Cakes. Or, you can simply mix and match using the squares from one Layer Cake to make each block unique.

CUTTING

Before cutting the 10" squares, choose 24 darker prints for the patchwork squares and 2 darker prints for the 2½" sashing squares. All measurements include ¼" seam allowances.

From *each* of 24 dark print squares, cut:
2 pieces, 4½" × 8½" (48 total)

From *each* of 2 dark print squares, cut:
10 squares, 2½" × 2½" (20 total)

From *each* of the 12 remaining dark print squares, cut:
4 squares, 5" × 5" (48 total)

From the white solid, cut:
18 strips, 4½" × 42"; crosscut into 144 squares, 4½" × 4½"
16 strips, 2½" × 42"; crosscut into 31 strips, 2½" × 16½"

From the teal solid, cut:
7 strips, 1½" × 42"

From the teal floral, cut:
8 strips, 3" × 42"

From the navy print, cut:
8 strips, 2½" × 42"

MAKING THE BLOCKS

Press seam allowances in the directions indicated by the arrows.

1 Draw a diagonal line from corner to corner on the wrong side of 96 white 4½" squares. Place a marked square on one end of a print piece, right sides together. Sew on the marked line. Trim the excess corner fabric ¼" from the stitched line. Place a marked square on the opposite end of the print piece. Sew and trim as before to make a flying-geese unit measuring 4½" × 8½", including seam allowances. Make 48 units.

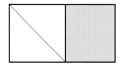
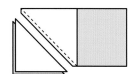
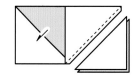
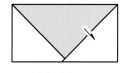

Make 48 units,
4½" × 8½".

2 Draw a diagonal line from corner to corner on the wrong side of 24 print 5" squares. Layer a marked square on a contrasting print 5" square, right sides together. Sew ¼" from both sides of the drawn line. Cut the unit apart on the marked line to make two half-square-triangle units. Trim the units to measure 4½" square, including seam allowances. Repeat to make 48 units.

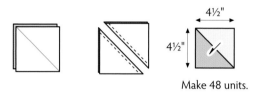

Make 48 units.

3 Lay out one flying-geese unit, one white 4½" square, and one half-square-triangle unit. Join the square and units to make a quarter-block unit measuring 8½" square, including seam allowances. Make 48 units.

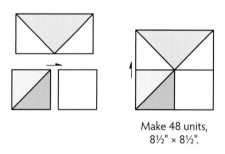

Make 48 units,
8½" × 8½".

4 Lay out four quarter-block units in two rows, rotating the units to form a pinwheel in the center. Sew the units into rows. Join the rows to make a block measuring 16½" square, including seam allowances. Make 12 blocks.

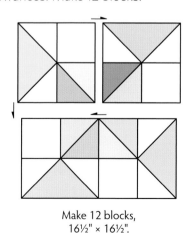

Make 12 blocks,
16½" × 16½".

sashing statement

Sometimes the sashing's job in a quilt layout is simply to let us avoid sewing points of one block to the points of another. But in Cartwheels and Roundoffs, adding the sashing cornerstones makes piecing easier *and* adds big impact, as those little squares create a whole new pinwheel as a secondary design.

ASSEMBLING THE QUILT TOP

1 Join four print 2½" squares and three white 2½" × 16½" strips to make a sashing row measuring 2½" × 56½", including seam allowances. Make five rows.

Make 5 sashing rows,
2½" × 56½".

2 Join four white 2½" × 16½" strips and three blocks to make a block row measuring 16½" × 56½", including seam allowances. Make four rows.

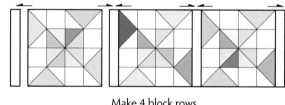

Make 4 block rows,
16½" × 56½".

3 Join the sashing rows alternately with the block rows, rotating every other sashing row as shown in the quilt assembly diagram on page 35. The quilt-top center should measure 56½" × 74½", including seam allowances.

4 Join the teal solid strips end to end. From the pieced strip, cut two 76½"-long strips and two 56½"-long strips. Sew the shorter strips to the top and bottom of the quilt center. Sew the longer strips to the left and right sides. The quilt top should measure 58½" × 76½", including seam allowances.

5 Join the teal floral strips end to end. From the pieced strip, cut two 81½"-long strips and two 58½"-long strips. Sew the shorter strips to the top and bottom of the quilt top. Sew the longer strips to the left and right sides to complete the quilt top. The quilt top should measure 63½" × 81½".

FINISHING THE QUILT

For more details on any finishing steps, visit ShopMartingale.com/HowtoQuilt for free downloadable information.

1 Layer the quilt top with batting and backing; baste the layers together.

2 Quilt by hand or machine. Lisa Jo's quilt is machine quilted with an allover design of leaves and flowers.

3 Use the navy 2½"-wide strips to make double-fold binding. Attach the binding to the quilt.

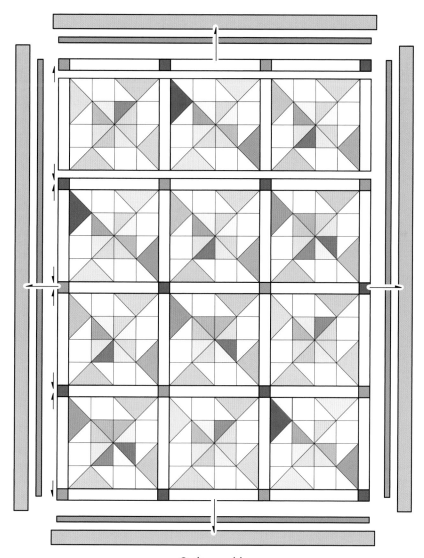

Quilt assembly

DAYNA

FROM THE KITCHEN OF: *sharla krenzel*

Sharla simply loves stars, chains, and plaid, and she's certainly not alone! Her stellar design combines all three of these elements, and the result is absolutely irresistible. Much easier than it looks, this design will have you reaching for the stars in no time!

FINISHED QUILT: 60½" × 60½"   **FINISHED BLOCKS: 6" × 6"**

MATERIALS

Yardage is based on 42"-wide fabric. A Moda Fabrics Layer Cake contains 42 squares, 10" × 10". Sharla used Happy Days by Sherri & Chelsi for Moda Fabrics. Divide your Layer Cake into like colors as noted below.

- 7 squares, 10" × 10", of red prints for Star blocks
- 5 squares, 10" × 10", of navy prints for Double Four Patch and Nine Patch blocks
- 17 squares, 10" × 10", of assorted prints for Nine Patch blocks, Strip blocks, and border

- 2½ yards of cream print for blocks and border
- ⅝ yard of navy diagonal stripe for binding
- 3¾ yards of fabric for backing
- 67" × 67" piece of batting

CUTTING

All measurements include ¼" seam allowances.

From 3 of the red print squares, cut a *total* of:
72 squares, 2" × 2"

From 4 of the red print squares, cut a *total* of:
13 squares, 3½" × 3½"
32 squares, 2" × 2"

From the navy print squares, cut a *total* of:
112 squares, 2" × 2"

From the assorted print squares, cut a *total* of:
80 strips, 2" x 10"; crosscut into:
    80 pieces, 2" × 6½"
    88 pieces, 2" × 3½"

From the cream print, cut:
6 strips, 2" × 42"; crosscut into 116 squares, 2" × 2"
19 strips, 3½" × 42"; crosscut into:
    56 pieces, 3½" × 6½"
    52 pieces, 2" × 3½"
    68 squares, 3½" × 3½"

From the navy diagonal stripe, cut:
7 strips, 2½" × 42"

MAKING THE STAR BLOCKS

Press seam allowances in the directions indicated by the arrows.

1 Draw a diagonal line from corner to corner on the wrong side of the red 2" squares. Place a marked square on one end of a cream 2" × 3½" piece, right sides together. Sew on the marked line. Trim the excess corner fabric ¼" from the stitched line. Place a matching marked square on the opposite end of the cream piece. Sew and trim as before to make a flying-geese unit measuring 2" × 3½", including seam allowances. Make 52 units.

Make 52 units,
2" × 3½".

2 Lay out four cream 2" squares, four matching flying-geese units, and one red 3½" square in three rows. Sew the squares and units into rows. Join the rows to make a Star block measuring 6½" square, including seam allowances. Make 13 blocks.

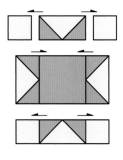 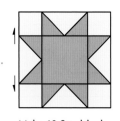

Make 13 Star blocks,
6½" × 6½".

MAKING THE DOUBLE FOUR PATCH BLOCKS

1 Lay out two navy and two cream 2" squares in two rows. Sew the squares into rows and then join the rows to make a four-patch unit measuring 3½" square, including seam allowances. Make 32 units.

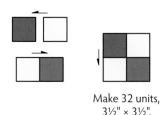

Make 32 units,
3½" × 3½".

2 Lay out two cream 3½" squares and two four-patch units in two rows. Sew the squares and units into rows. Join the rows to make a Double Four Patch block measuring 6½" square, including seam allowances. Make 16 blocks.

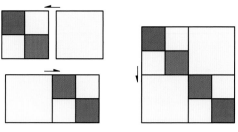

Make 16 Double Four Patch blocks,
6½" × 6½".

MAKING THE NINE PATCH BLOCKS

Lay out four navy squares, four assorted print 2" × 3½" pieces, and one cream 3½" square in three rows. Sew the pieces into rows. Join the rows to make a Nine Patch block measuring 6½" square, including seam allowances. Make 12 blocks.

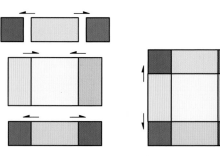

Make 12 Nine Patch blocks,
6½" × 6½".

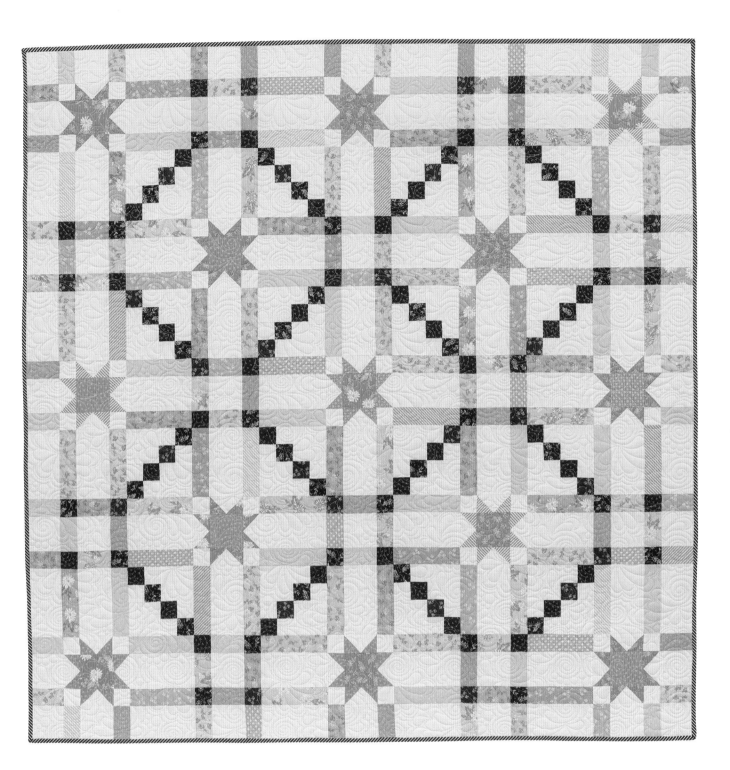

mix it up

To distribute the various colors of the assorted prints evenly throughout the quilt, make each of the Nine Patch blocks using 2" × 3½" pieces in four different colors. Then before assembling the Strip blocks, lay out all of the blocks as shown in the quilt assembly diagram on page 41 to determine the color placement of the print 2" × 6½" pieces in the Strip blocks and border units.

MAKING THE STRIP BLOCKS

Join two print 2" × 6½" pieces and one cream 3½" × 6½" piece to make a Strip block. Make 40 blocks measuring 6½" square, including seam allowances.

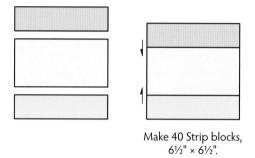

Make 40 Strip blocks,
6½" × 6½".

ASSEMBLING THE QUILT TOP

Refer to the quilt assembly diagram as needed throughout.

1 Join two print 2" × 3½" pieces and one cream 3½" square to make a border unit. Make 20 units measuring 3½" × 6½", including seam allowances.

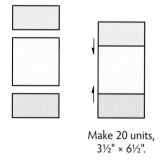

Make 20 units,
3½" × 6½".

2 Join two cream 3½" squares, five border units, and four cream 3½" × 6½" pieces to make row A. Make two rows.

3 Join two border units, three Star blocks, four Strip blocks, and two Nine Patch blocks to make row B. Make three rows.

4 Join two cream 3½" × 6½" pieces, five Strip blocks, and four Double Four Patch blocks to make row C. Make four rows.

5 Join two border units, three Nine Patch blocks, four Strip blocks, and two Star blocks to make row D. Make two rows.

6 Lay out the rows, rotating row C as needed to form a chain of squares. Join the rows to complete the quilt top. The quilt top should measure 60½" square, including seam allowances.

FINISHING THE QUILT

For more details on any finishing steps, visit ShopMartingale.com/HowtoQuilt for free downloadable information.

1 Layer the quilt top with batting and backing; baste the layers together.

2 Quilt by hand or machine. Sharla's quilt is machine quilted with an allover design of feathers, swirls, and pearls.

3 Use the navy diagonal stripe 2½"-wide strips to make double-fold binding. Attach the binding to the quilt.

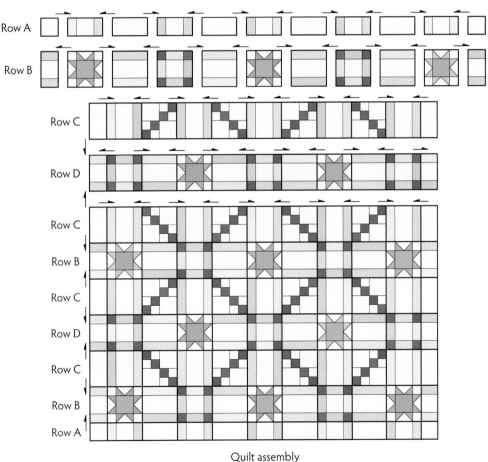

Quilt assembly

BLOSSOM

FROM THE KITCHEN OF: *nicola dodd*

Combine your favorite Layer Cake with simple piecing to evoke a fresh spring day—a soft breeze carrying the scent of blossoms and the gentle hum of busy bumblebees. Don't worry—these bees won't sting! They are simply doing their job to pollinate all the pretty flowers in your garden. Blossom is nature at its best!

FINISHED QUILT: 50½" × 50½"   **FINISHED BLOCKS: 10" × 10"**

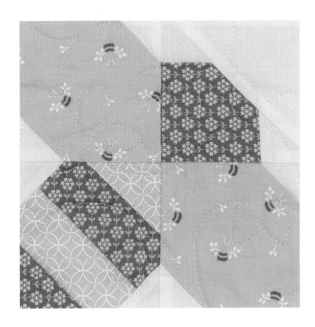

MATERIALS

Yardage is based on 42"-wide fabric. A Moda Fabrics Layer Cake contains 42 squares, 10" × 10". Nicola used Spring Brook by Corey Yoder and Bella Solids, both for Moda Fabrics.

- 6 squares, 10" × 10", of blue prints for Blossom blocks
- 5 squares, 10" × 10", of yellow print for Blossom and Bumblebee blocks
- 4 squares, 10" × 10", of green prints for Blossom blocks

- 2 squares, 10" × 10", of gray prints for Bumblebee blocks
- 4 squares, 10" × 10", of taupe prints for Bumblebee blocks
- 3 yards of white solid for blocks
- ½ yard of green print for binding
- 3¼ yards of fabric for backing
- 57" × 57" piece of batting

CUTTING

All measurements include ¼" seam allowances.

From *each* of the blue print squares, cut:
24 pieces, 1½" × 2½" (144 total; 16 are extra)

From *each* of 3 yellow print squares, cut:
11 squares, 2½" × 2½" (33 total, 1 is extra)

From *each* of 2 yellow print squares, cut:
2 squares, 4" × 4" (4 total)
4 squares, 2" × 2" (8 total)

From *each* of the green print squares, cut:
8 pieces, 2½" × 4½" (32 total)

From *each* of the gray print squares, cut:
2 squares, 4" × 4" (4 total)
4 squares, 2½" × 2½" (8 total)
4 squares, 2" × 2" (8 total)

Continued on page 44

Continued from page 43

From *each* of the taupe print squares, cut:

4 squares, 3½" × 3½" (16 total)

From the white solid, cut:

7 strips, 4½" × 42"; crosscut *2 of the strips* into
    8 pieces, 4½" × 6½"

1 strip, 3½" × 42"; crosscut into 8 squares,
    3½" × 3½"

14 strips, 2½" × 42"; crosscut *12 of the strips* into:
    2 strips, 2½" × 20½"
    8 strips, 2½" × 10½"
    24 pieces, 2½" × 4½"
    64 squares, 2½" × 2½"

7 strips, 2" × 42"; crosscut into 128 squares, 2" × 2"

9 strips, 1½" × 42"; crosscut into:
    8 pieces, 1½" × 3½"
    8 pieces, 1½" × 2½"
    176 squares, 1½" × 1½"

From the green print for binding, cut:

6 strips, 2½" × 42"

MAKING THE BLOSSOM BLOCKS

Press seam allowances in the directions indicated by the arrows.

1 Lay out four white 1½" squares, four blue 1½" × 2½" pieces, and one yellow 2½" square in three rows. Sew the squares and pieces into rows. Join the rows to make a nine-patch unit measuring 4½" square, including seam allowances. Make 32 units.

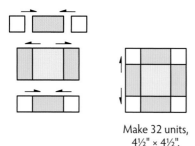

Make 32 units,
4½" × 4½".

2 Draw a diagonal line from corner to corner on the wrong side of the white 2" squares. Place a marked square on one corner of a unit from step 1. Sew on the marked line. Trim the excess corner fabric ¼" from the stitched line. Place marked squares on the remaining corners of the unit. Sew and trim as before to make a petal unit measuring 4½" square, including seam allowances. Make 32 units.

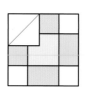

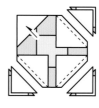

Make 32 petal units,
4½" × 4½".

3 Draw a diagonal line from corner to corner on the wrong side of the white 2½" squares. Place a marked square on one end of a green piece, right sides together. Sew on the marked line. Trim the excess corner fabric ¼" from the stitched line. Place a marked square on the opposite end of the green piece, noting the direction of the marked line. Sew and trim as before to make a leaf unit measuring 2½" × 4½", including seam allowances. Make 32 units.

Make 32 leaf units,
2½" × 4½".

4 Sew a leaf unit to the right edge of a petal unit to make a unit measuring 4½" × 6½", including seam allowances. Make 32 units.

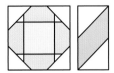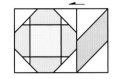

Make 32 units,
4½" × 6½".

5 Lay out one white 2½" × 4½" piece and three units from step 4 in two rows, noting the orientation of the petal/leaf units. Sew the pieces into rows. Join the rows. Sew a white 2½" × 10½" strip to the right edge to make a Blossom block measuring 10½" square, including seam allowances. Make eight. You'll have eight petal/leaf units left over for the Bumblebee blocks.

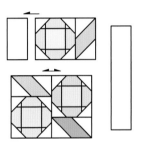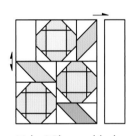

Make 8 Blossom blocks,
10½" × 10½".

MAKING THE BUMBLEBEE BLOCKS

1 Draw a diagonal line from corner to corner on the wrong side of the yellow 4" squares. Layer a marked square on a gray 4" square, right sides together. Sew ¼" from both sides of the drawn line. Cut the unit apart on the marked line to make two half-square-triangle units. Trim the units to measure 3½" square, including seam allowances. Make eight units.

Make 8 units.

2 Draw a diagonal line from corner to corner on the wrong side of the gray and yellow 2" squares. Layer a marked yellow square on the gray triangle of a unit from step 1. Sew on the marked line. Trim the excess corner fabric ¼" from the stitched line. Place a marked brown square on the yellow triangle. Sew and trim as before to make a unit measuring 3½" square, including seam allowances. Make eight units.

Make 8 units,
3½" × 3½".

3 Draw a diagonal line from corner to corner on the wrong side of the remaining white 1½" squares. Place marked squares on opposite corners of a unit from step 2. Sew on the marked lines. Trim the excess corner fabric ¼" from the stitched lines. Make eight body units measuring 3½" square, including seam allowances.

Make 8 body units,
3½" × 3½".

4 Place marked white squares from step 3 on opposite corners of a taupe square. Sew on the marked lines. Trim the excess corner fabric ¼" from the stitched lines. Make 16 wing units measuring 3½" square, including seam allowances.

Make 16 wing units,
3½" × 3½".

5 Sew a white 1½" × 2½" piece to a gray 2½" square. Add a white 1½" × 3½" piece to an adjacent side to make a head unit. Make eight units measuring 3½" square, including seam allowances.

Make 8 head units,
3½" × 3½".

6 Lay out one body unit, two wing units, and one head unit in two rows. Sew the units into rows. Join the rows to make a unit measuring 6½" square, including seam allowances. Make eight units.

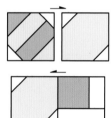 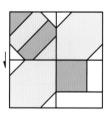

Make 8 units,
6½" × 6½".

7 Draw a diagonal line from corner to corner on the wrong side of the white 3½" squares. Place a marked square on top of a head unit, right sides together and raw edges aligned. Sew on the marked line. Trim the excess corner fabric ¼" from the stitched line. Make eight bee units measuring 6½" square, including seam allowances.

Make 8 bee units,
6½" × 6½".

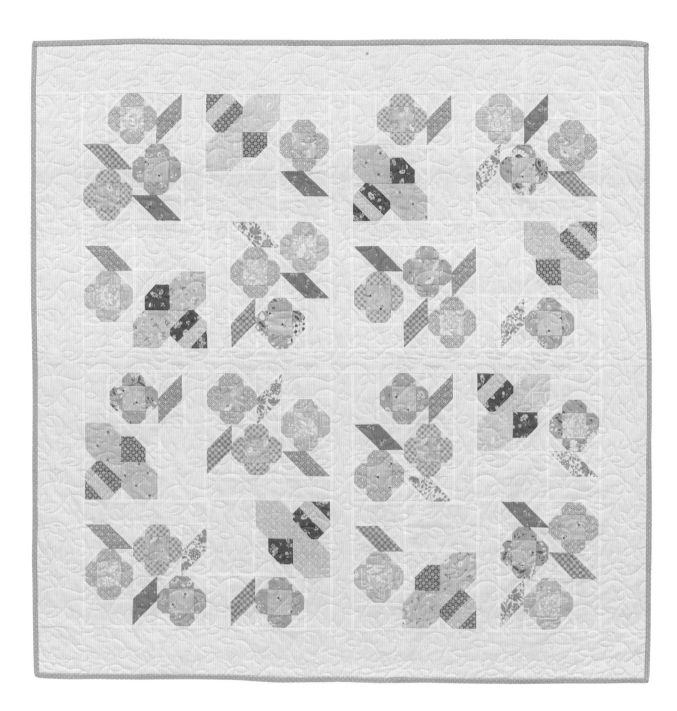

8 Lay out one bee unit, one white 4½" × 6½" piece, two white 2½" × 4½" pieces, and one petal/leaf unit, noting the orientation of the units. Sew the pieces into rows. Join the rows to make a Bumblebee block measuring 10½" square, including seam allowances. Make eight blocks.

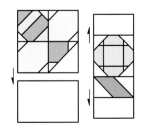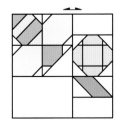

Make 8 Bumblebee blocks,
10½" × 10½".

ASSEMBLING THE QUILT TOP

1 Lay out two Blossom and two Bumblebee blocks in two rows, rotating the blocks as shown. Sew the blocks into rows. Join the rows to make a quadrant measuring 20½" square, including seam allowances. Make four quadrants.

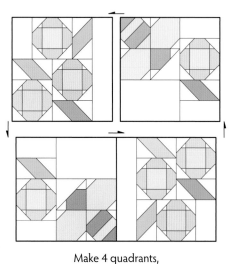

Make 4 quadrants,
20½" × 20½".

pressing matters

When assembling the blocks, you can create opposing seams and reduce bulk where the four seams meet. After sewing the rows together, use a seam ripper to remove one or two stitches from the seam allowance. Gently reposition the seam allowances to evenly distribute the fabric. Press the seam allowances in opposite directions.

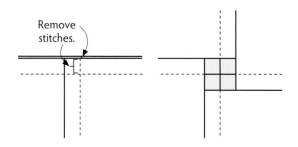

Remove stitches.

2 Join the remaining white 2½"-wide strips end to end. From the pieced strip, cut one 42½"-long sashing strip.

3 Join two quadrants and one white 2½" × 20½" strip to make a block row as shown in the quilt assembly diagram below. Make two rows.

4 Join the block rows and sashing strip from step 2 to make the quilt-top center, which should measure 42½" square, including seam allowances.

5 Join the remaining white 4½"-wide strips end to end. From the pieced strip, cut two 50½"-long strips and two 42½"-long strips. Sew the shorter strips to opposite sides of the quilt center. Sew the longer strips to the top and bottom edges to complete the quilt top. The quilt top should measure 50½" square.

FINISHING THE QUILT

For more details on any finishing steps, visit ShopMartingale.com/HowtoQuilt for free downloadable information.

1 Layer the quilt top with batting and backing; baste the layers together.

2 Quilt by hand or machine. Nicola's quilt is machine quilted by Jayne Brereton using an allover design of curved lines and leaves.

3 Use the green 2½"-wide strips to make double-fold binding. Attach the binding to the quilt.

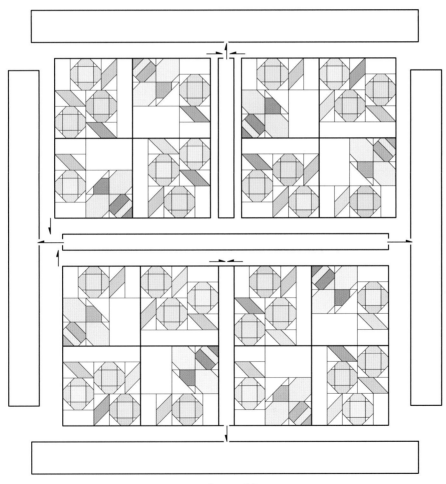

Quilt assembly

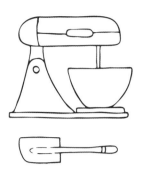

COTTAGE GARDEN

FROM THE KITCHEN OF: *jessica dayon*

Nothing says "cheerful" like a crop of cross-stitch-style X blocks surrounded by a ring of patchwork posies. Reminiscent of those printed tablecloths that were so popular in the 1940s and 1950s, Cottage Garden simply exudes a happy vibe. On a table, on a bed, or as a throw, this quilt is pure sunshine!

FINISHED QUILT: 74½" × 74½"   **FINISHED BLOCKS: 11¼" × 11¼" (cross) and 5" × 5" (flower)**

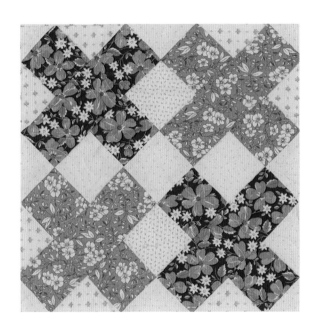

MATERIALS

Yardage is based on 42"-wide fabric. A Moda Fabrics Layer Cake contains 42 squares, 10" × 10". Jessica used 30's Playtime by Chloe's Closet for Moda Fabrics.

- 32 squares, 10" × 10", of assorted medium and dark prints (collectively referred to as "dark") for blocks
- 3 yards *total* of assorted white prints for blocks and pieced border
- ½ yard of green print for Flower blocks
- ½ yard of white dot for first border

- ¾ yard of white floral for third border
- 1⅛ yards of yellow print for fourth border
- ⅝ yard of navy print for binding
- 6¾ yards of fabric for backing
- 81" × 81" piece of batting

CUTTING

All measurements include ¼" seam allowances.

From the assorted white prints, cut a *total* of:

4 squares, 5½" × 5½"

48 squares, 4" × 4". Cut the squares into quarters diagonally to yield 192 A triangles.

80 squares, 3⅜" × 3⅜". Cut the squares in half diagonally to yield 160 D triangles.

40 squares, 2⅝" × 2⅝". Cut the squares in half diagonally to yield 80 C triangles.

80 squares, 2½" × 2½"

32 squares, 2¼" × 2¼". Cut the squares in half diagonally to yield 64 B triangles.

80 squares, 2" × 2"

From *each* of the dark print squares, cut:

2 pieces, 2½" × 6½" (64 total)
4 squares, 2½" × 2½" (128 total)

From the remaining dark prints cut a *total* of:

40 squares, 2¼" x 2¼"

Continued on page 52

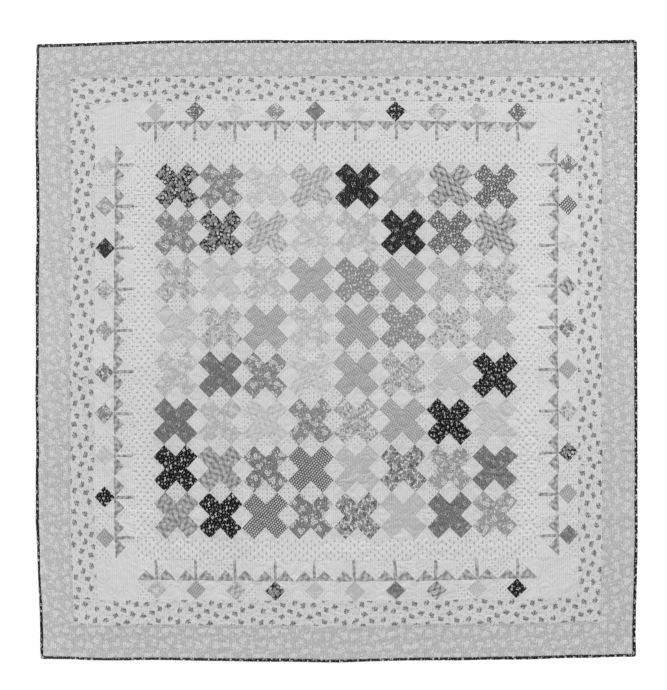

Continued from page 51

From the white dot, cut:
5 strips, 3" × 42"

From the white floral, cut:
7 strips, 3½" × 42"

From the yellow print, cut:
8 strips, 4½" × 42"

From the navy print, cut:
8 strips, 2½" × 42"

From the green print, cut:
3 strips, 2¼" × 42"; crosscut into 40 squares,
    2¼" × 2¼"
3 strips, 2⅝" × 42"; crosscut into 40 squares,
    2⅝" × 2⅝". Cut the squares in half diagonally
    to yield 80 triangles.

MAKING THE CROSS BLOCKS

Press seam allowances in the directions indicated by the arrows.

1 For each block, select the following pieces. Repeat to choose pieces for 16 blocks.

- **Dark print 1:** four 2½" squares and two 2½" × 6½" pieces

- **Dark print 2:** four 2½" squares and two 2½" × 6½" pieces

- **Assorted white prints:** five 2½" squares, 12 A triangles, and four B triangles

2 Lay out and sew the squares, pieces, and triangles in diagonal rows, according to the diagram. Join the rows to make a Cross block measuring 11¾" square, including seam allowances. Make 16 blocks.

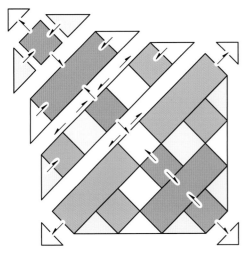

Make 16 Cross blocks,
11¾" × 11¾".

MAKING THE FLOWER BLOCKS

1 Sew a white print C triangle to the long side of a green triangle to make a half-square-triangle unit. Make 80 units measuring 2¼" square, including seam allowances.

Make 80 units,
2¼" × 2¼".

2 Draw a diagonal line from corner to corner on the wrong side of the white print 2" squares. Place a marked square on one corner of a green 2¼" square, right sides together. Sew on the marked line. Trim the excess corner fabric ¼" from the stitched line. Place a marked square on the opposite corner of the green square. Sew and trim as before to make a stem unit measuring 2¼" square, including seam allowances. Make 40 units.

Make 40 units,
2¼" × 2¼".

3 Lay out two half-square-triangle units, one stem unit, and one dark 2¼" square in two rows. Sew the units and square into rows. Join the rows to make a unit measuring 4" square, including seam allowances. Make 40 units.

Make 40 units,
4" × 4".

4 Center and sew white print D triangles to opposite corners of a unit from step 3. Sew D triangles to the remaining two corners to make a Flower block measuring 5½" square, including seam allowances. Make 40 blocks.

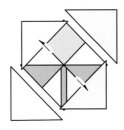 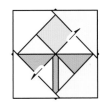

Make 40 Flower blocks,
5½" × 5½".

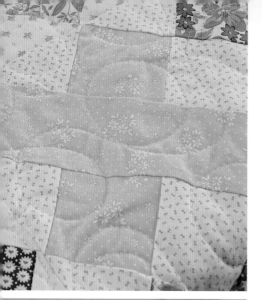

ASSEMBLING THE QUILT-TOP CENTER

Lay out the Cross blocks in four rows of four blocks each as shown in the quilt assembly diagram. Sew the blocks into rows. Join the rows to make the quilt-top center, which should measure 45½" square, including seam allowances.

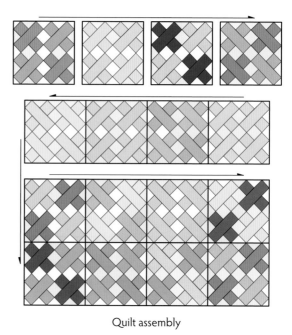

Quilt assembly

ADDING THE BORDERS

1 Join the white dot 3"-wide strips end to end. From the pieced strip, cut two 50½"-long strips and two 45½"-long strips. Sew the shorter strips to opposite sides of the quilt center. Sew the longer strips to the top and bottom edges. The quilt top should measure 50½" square, including seam allowances.

2 Join 10 Flower blocks to make a side border measuring 5½" × 50½", including seam allowances. Make two. Make two more borders in the same way, and add a white print 5½" square to each end. The top and bottom borders should measure 5½" × 60½", including seam allowances.

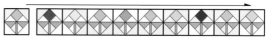

Make 2 side borders, 5½" × 50½".

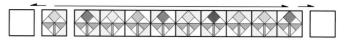

Make 2 top/bottom borders, 5½" × 60½".

3 Sew the shorter flower borders to opposite sides of the quilt top. Sew the longer flower borders to the top and bottom edges. The quilt top should measure 60½", including seam allowances.

4 Join the white floral 3½"-wide strips end to end. From the pieced strip, cut two 66½"-long strips and two 60½"-long strips. Sew the shorter strips to opposite sides of the quilt center. Sew the longer strips to the top and bottom edges. The quilt top should measure 66½" square, including seam allowances.

5 Join the yellow strips end to end. From the pieced strip, cut two 74½"-long strips and two 66½"-long strips. Sew the shorter strips to opposite sides of the quilt center. Sew the longer strips to the top and bottom edges to complete the quilt top, which should measure 74½" square.

FINISHING THE QUILT

For more details on any finishing steps, visit ShopMartingale.com/HowtoQuilt for free downloadable information.

1 Layer the quilt top with batting and backing; baste the layers together.

2 Quilt by hand or machine. Jessica's quilt is machine quilted with an allover swirl design.

3 Use the navy 2½"-wide strips to make double-fold binding. Attach the binding to the quilt.

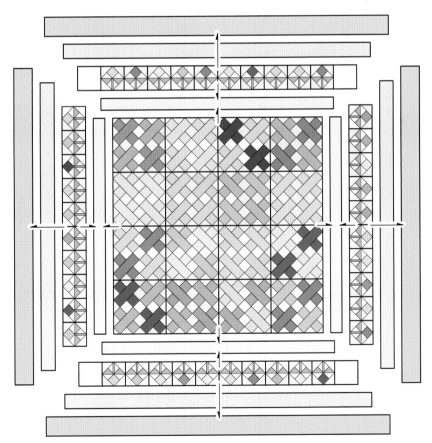

Adding borders

MOUNTAINTOP

FROM THE KITCHEN OF: *lauren elizabeth terry*

Frequently quiltmakers combine a Bella Solid Layer Cake with a print one to make cutting and sewing blocks a breeze. But it's not very often you see two high-contrast solid Layer Cakes combined into a graphic and fun quilt pattern. Will your mountains be all solids too? Or are prints calling your name?

FINISHED QUILT: 51½" × 64¼"   **FINISHED BLOCKS: 9" × 9"**

MATERIALS

Yardage is based on 42"-wide fabric. A Moda Fabrics Layer Cake contains 42 squares, 10" × 10". Lauren used Bella Solids by Moda Fabrics.

- 49 squares, 10" × 10", of navy solid for blocks
- 42 squares, 10" × 10", of white solid for blocks
- ⅝ yard of navy solid for binding
- 3¼ yards of fabric for backing
- 58" × 71" piece of batting

CUTTING

Refer to the cutting chart below for cutting the navy squares and the charts on page 58 for cutting the white squares to yield the quantities listed below and to make the best use of your fabrics. All measurements include ¼" seam allowances.

From the navy solid squares, cut:
49 strips, 2" × 9½" (H)
49 strips, 2" × 8" (G)
49 strips, 2" × 6½" (D)
49 strips, 2" × 5" (C)
49 squares, 3½" × 3½"

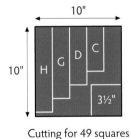

Cutting for 49 squares

Continued on page 58

Continued from page 57

From the white solid squares, cut:

49 strips, 2" × 8" (F)

49 strips, 2" × 6½" (E)

49 strips, 2" × 5" (B)

49 strips, 2" × 3½" (A)

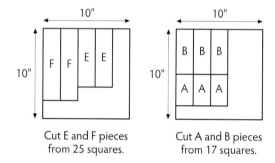

Cut E and F pieces from 25 squares.

Cut A and B pieces from 17 squares.

From the navy solid for binding, cut:

7 strips, 2½" × 42"

MAKING THE BLOCKS

Press seam allowances in the directions indicated by the arrows.

1 Sew a white A strip to the left edge of a navy square. Sew a white B strip to the top edge to make a unit measuring 5" square, including seam allowances. Make 49 units.

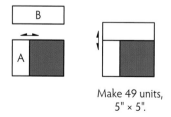

Make 49 units, 5" × 5".

2 Sew a navy C strip to the left edge of the unit from step 1. Sew a navy D strip to the top edge to make a unit measuring 6½" square, including seam allowances. Make 49 units.

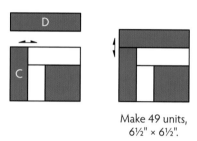

Make 49 units, 6½" × 6½".

3 Sew a white E strip to the left edge of the unit. Sew a white F strip to the top edge to make a unit measuring 8" square, including seam allowances. Make 49 units.

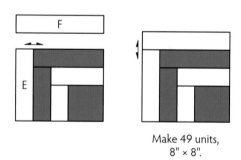

Make 49 units, 8" × 8".

4 Sew a navy G strip to the left edge of the unit. Sew a navy H strip to the top edge to make a block measuring 9½" square, including seam allowances. Make 49 blocks.

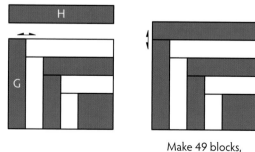

Make 49 blocks, 9½" × 9½".

ASSEMBLING THE QUILT TOP

1 Referring to the quilt assembly diagram below, lay out the blocks in nine diagonal rows. Sew the blocks into rows, and then join the rows.

2 Trim and square up the quilt top, making sure to leave ¼" beyond the points of all blocks for seam allowances. The quilt top should measure 51½" × 64¼".

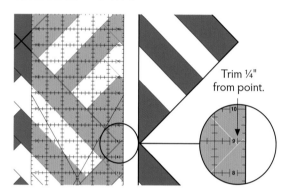

Trim ¼" from point.

3 Stitch around the perimeter of the quilt top, ⅛" from the outer edges, to prevent the bias edges from stretching and to lock the seams in place.

FINISHING THE QUILT

For more details on any finishing steps, visit ShopMartingale.com/HowtoQuilt for free downloadable information.

1 Layer the quilt top with batting and backing; baste the layers together.

2 Quilt by hand or machine. Lauren's quilt is machine quilted with an allover design of elongated loops.

3 Use the navy 2½"-wide strips to make double-fold binding and then attach the binding to the quilt.

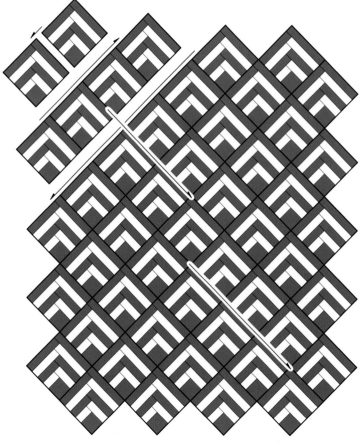

Quilt assembly

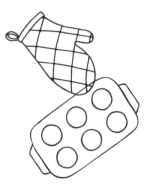

BATTENBERG

FROM THE KITCHEN OF: *julie hirt*

Named for the famed British Battenberg cake, the four patches in the quilt design resemble the checkerboard design of the cake. While patchwork blocks may not satisfy your sweet tooth, we're betting they're easier to assemble than the cake and the quilt is sure to add more than a dash of fun to your decor.

FINISHED QUILT: 58½" × 72½"   **FINISHED BLOCKS: 12" × 12"**

MATERIALS

Yardage is based on 42"-wide fabric. A Moda Fabrics Layer Cake contains 42 squares, 10" × 10". Julie used Smol by Ruby Star Society for Moda Fabrics.

- 40 squares, 10" × 10", of assorted prints for blocks
- 1⅓ yards of light print for sashing
- ¾ yard of navy print for sashing squares and binding
- 3⅝ yards of fabric for backing
- 65" × 79" piece of batting

CUTTING

All measurements include ¼" seam allowances.

From the light print, cut:
17 strips, 2½" × 42"; crosscut into 49 strips, 2½" × 12½"

From the navy print, cut:
9 strips, 2½" × 42"; crosscut *2 of the strips* into 30 squares, 2½" × 2½"

MAKING THE BLOCKS

Divide the print 10" squares into two groups with 20 light squares in one group and 20 dark squares in the other group. Label the light prints as group A and label the dark prints as group B. Press seam allowances in the directions indicated by the arrows.

1 Pair two contrasting A squares; make 10 pairs.

2 Layer one pair of A squares right sides together. On the wrong side of the top square, draw a line across the center of the square as shown in the illustration on page 63. Sew ¼" from both sides of the drawn line. Cut the squares

apart on the marked line to make two units measuring 9½" × 10", including seam allowances.

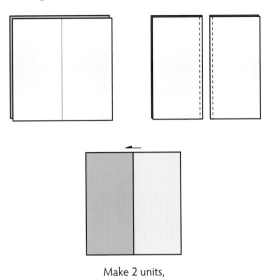

Make 2 units,
9½" × 10".

3 Rotate each unit 90°. Cut the units in half to make four identical two-patch units measuring 5" × 9½", including seam allowances.

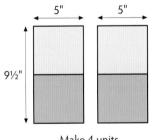

Make 4 units.

4 Join two matching units to make a four-patch unit. Make two units and trim them to measure 9" square, including seam allowances. Repeat the steps to make a total of 20 units.

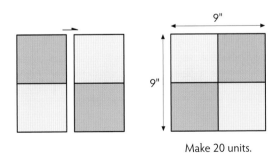

Make 20 units.

5 Cut each group B square into quarters diagonally to yield 10 sets of four triangles.

Cut 10 sets of 4 triangles.

6 Using one set of triangles, center and sew triangles to opposite sides of a four-patch unit. Center and sew triangles to the remaining sides of the unit to make a block. Trim the block, making sure to leave ¼" beyond the points of the four patch for seam allowances. Make 20 blocks measuring 12½" square, including seam allowances.

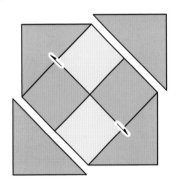

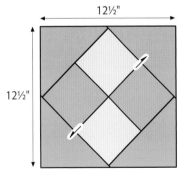

Make 20 blocks.

Did Somebody Say Cake?

ASSEMBLING THE QUILT TOP

1 Join five navy squares and four light strips to make a sashing row measuring 2½" × 58½", including seam allowances. Make six sashing rows.

2 Join five light strips and four blocks to make a block row measuring 12½" × 58½", including seam allowances. Make five block rows.

3 Join the sashing rows and blocks rows in alternating positions as shown in the quilt assembly diagram. The quilt top should measure 58½" × 72½".

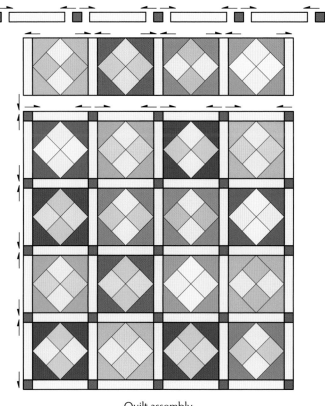

Quilt assembly

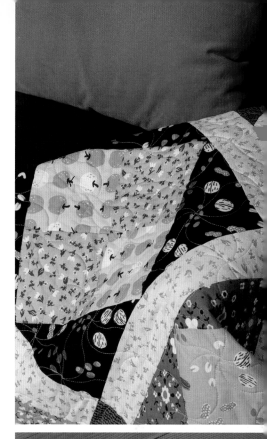

FINISHING THE QUILT

For more details on any finishing steps, find free downloadable information at ShopMartingale.com/HowtoQuilt.

1 Layer the quilt top with batting and backing; baste the layers together.

2 Quilt by hand or machine. Julie's quilt is machine quilted with an allover design of intersecting curved lines.

3 Use the remaining navy 2½"-wide strips to make double-fold binding. Attach the binding to the quilt.

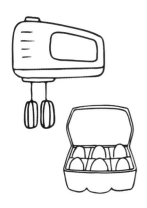

FIELD AND FLOCK

FROM THE KITCHEN OF: *christine weld*

Checkerboards and flying geese, two favorites among quilters, come together in a quilt that can easily be adapted to your favorite fabric collection. The geese fly around the Checkerboard blocks in alternating directions in a design that is surprisingly simple to construct.

FINISHED QUILT: 64½" × 64½"   **FINISHED BLOCKS: 10" × 10"**

MATERIALS

Yardage is based on 42"-wide fabric. A Moda Fabrics Layer Cake contains 42 squares, 10" × 10". Christine used Sunday Stroll by Bonnie and Camille for Moda Fabrics.

- 40 squares, 10" × 10", of assorted prints for blocks and sashing
- 4¼ yards of gray solid for blocks, sashing, and border
- ⅝ yard of navy stripe for binding
- 4 yards of fabric for backing
- 71" × 71" piece of batting

CUTTING

Refer to the cutting diagram below as needed to cut the 10" squares. Cut the squares carefully, as you will not have any leftover fabric. All measurements include ¼" seam allowances.

From *each* of the assorted print squares, cut:
5 pieces, 2½" × 4½" (200 total)
5 squares, 2½" × 2½" (200 total; 8 are extra)

Cutting for 10" squares

From the gray solid, cut:
48 strips, 2½" × 42"; crosscut *41 of the strips* into 608 squares, 2½" × 2½"
4 strips, 4½" × 42"; crosscut into 25 squares, 4½" × 4½"

From the navy stripe, cut:
7 strips, 2½" × 42"

67

MAKING THE BLOCKS

Press seam allowances in the directions indicated by the arrows.

Lay out 13 gray 2½" squares and 12 different print squares in five rows of five squares. Sew the squares into rows. Join the rows to make a Checkerboard block measuring 10½" square, including seam allowances. Make 16 blocks.

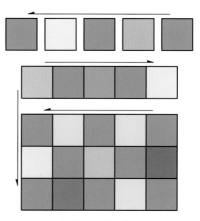

Make 16 blocks,
10½" × 10½".

MAKING THE SASHING

1 Draw a diagonal line from corner to corner on the wrong side of the remaining gray 2½" squares. Place a marked square on one end of a print piece, right sides together. Sew on the marked line. Trim the excess corner fabric ¼" from the stitched line. Place a marked square on the opposite end of the print piece. Sew and trim as before to make a flying-geese unit measuring 2½" × 4½", including seam allowances. Make 200 units.

Make 200 units,
2½" × 4½".

2 Join five flying-geese units to make a sashing unit, noting the pressing directions for the seam allowances. Make 20 A units measuring 4½" × 10½", including seam allowances. Repeat to make 20 B units, pressing the seam allowances in the opposite direction.

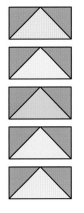 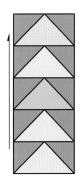 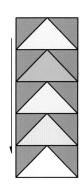

Make 20 A units, 4½" × 10½".

Make 20 B units, 4½" × 10½".

ASSEMBLING THE QUILT TOP

1 Join five gray 4½" squares, two A sashing units, and two B sashing units, noting the orientation of the units. Make three sashing rows that start with an A unit. Make two sashing rows that start with a B unit. The sashing rows should measure 4½" × 60½", including seam allowances.

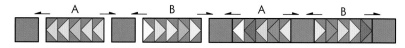

Make 3 sashing rows,
4½" × 60½".

Make 2 sashing rows,
4½" × 60½".

2 Join three B sashing units, two A sashing units, and four Checkerboard blocks to make a block row, noting the orientation of the units. Make two block rows. Make two more block rows using three A sashing units, two B sashing units, and four Checkerboard blocks. The block rows should measure 10½" × 60½", including seam allowances.

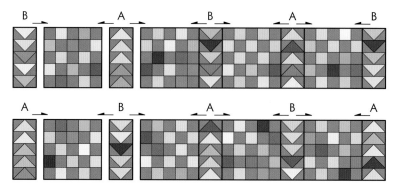

Make 2 of each block rows,
10½" × 60½".

3 Join the sashing rows and block rows as shown in the quilt assembly diagram below, paying careful attention to the orientation of the flying-geese units. The quilt-top center should measure 60½" square, including seam allowances.

4 Join the remaining gray 2½"-wide strips end to end. From the pieced strip, cut two 64½"-long strips and two 60½"-long strips. Sew the shorter strips to opposite sides of the quilt center. Sew the longer strips to the top and bottom edges to complete the quilt top. The quilt top should measure 64½" square.

FINISHING THE QUILT

For more details on any finishing steps, visit ShopMartingale.com/HowtoQuilt for free downloadable information.

1 Layer the quilt top with batting and backing; baste the layers together.

2 Quilt by hand or machine. Christine's quilt was machine quilted by Lisa Jo Girodat using an allover pattern of swirls and leaves.

3 Use the navy 2½"-wide strips to make double-fold binding. Attach the binding to the quilt.

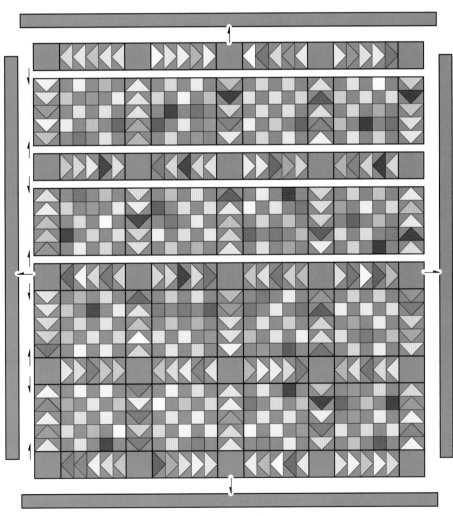

Quilt assembly

FRIENDS FOREVER

FROM THE KITCHEN OF: *Susan vaughan*

Through the years and across the miles, friends find a way to stay connected—just like these updated Friendship Stars. Grab your favorite Layer Cake and make blocks in your favorite color or style. Before you know it, you'll have a throw-sized quilt to wrap around yourself just like a hug from a good friend!

FINISHED QUILT: 62" × 62"   FINISHED BLOCKS: 12" × 12"

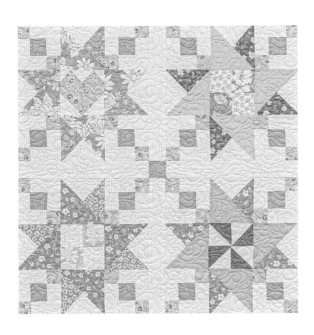

MATERIALS

Yardage is based on 42"-wide fabric. A Moda Fabrics Layer Cake contains 42 squares, 10" × 10". Susan used Strawberries and Rhubarb by Fig Tree & Co. for Moda Fabrics.

- 32 squares, 10" × 10", of assorted dark prints for blocks
- 8 squares, 10" × 10", of assorted light prints for blocks
- 2½ yards of ivory solid for blocks, sashing, and inner border
- ⅜ yard of rose print for blocks

- ⅓ yard of green print for blocks and sashing
- ¾ yard of green floral for outer border
- ⅝ yard of coral print for binding
- 3⅞ yards of fabric for backing
- 68" × 68" piece of batting

CUTTING

All measurements include ¼" seam allowances.

From *each* of 16 dark print squares, cut:
2 squares, 5" × 5"; cut the squares in half diagonally to yield 4 A triangles (64 total)
2 squares, 4" × 4"; cut the squares in half diagonally to yield 4 B triangles (64 total)

From the remaining 16 dark print squares, cut a *total* of:
4 pairs (8 total) of matching squares, 3" × 3" (pinwheel units)
4 squares, 3" × 3" (butterfly units)
4 pairs (8 total) of matching squares, 2½" × 2½" (four-patch units)
4 pairs (8 total) of matching pieces, 2½" × 4½" (heart units)

From 4 of the light print squares, cut a *total* of:
4 pairs (8 total) of matching squares, 2½" × 2½" (four-patch units)

Continued on page 74

Continued from page 73

From *each* of 4 light print squares, cut:

1 pair of matching squares, 2½" × 2½" (butterfly units; 4 pairs total)

1 square, 3" × 3" (butterfly units; 4 total)

From the ivory solid, cut:

4 strips, 4" × 42"; crosscut into 32 squares, 4" × 4". Cut the squares in half diagonally to yield 64 triangles.

6 strips, 3¼" × 42"; crosscut into 128 pieces, 1¾" × 3¼"

1 strip, 3" × 42"; crosscut into 8 squares, 3" × 3"

1 strip, 2½" × 42"; crosscut into 8 squares, 2½" × 2½"

8 strips, 2" × 42"; crosscut into 24 strips, 2" × 12½"

7 strips, 1¾" × 42"; crosscut into 128 pieces, 1¾" × 2"

7 strips, 1½" × 42"; crosscut *1 of the strips* into 16 squares, 1½" × 1½"

From the rose print, cut:

6 strips, 1¾" × 42"; crosscut into 128 squares, 1¾" × 1¾"

From the green print, cut:

4 strips, 2" × 42"; crosscut into 73 squares, 2" × 2"

From the green floral, cut:

6 strips, 4" × 42"

From the coral print, cut:

7 strips, 2½" × 42"

MAKING THE CENTER UNITS

Press seam allowances in the directions indicated by the arrows.

Four-Patch Units

Lay out two matching dark 2½" squares and two matching light 2½" squares in two rows. Sew the squares into rows. Join the rows to make a four-patch unit. Make four units measuring 4½" square, including seam allowances.

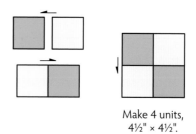

Make 4 units,
4½" × 4½".

Butterfly Units

1 Draw a diagonal line from corner to corner on the wrong side of a light 3" square. Layer a marked square on a dark 3" square, right sides together. Sew ¼" from both sides of the drawn line. Cut the unit apart on the marked line to make two half-square-triangle units. Trim the units to measure 2½" square, including seam allowances. Make eight matching triangle units.

Make 8 matching units.

2 Lay out two matching triangle units and two light 2½" squares in two rows. The light print should be the same throughout. Sew the units and squares into rows. Join the rows to make a butterfly unit. Make four units measuring 4½" square, including seam allowances.

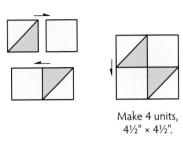

Make 4 units,
4½" × 4½".

Pinwheel Units

1 Draw a diagonal line from corner to corner on the wrong side of the ivory 3" squares. Layer a marked square on a dark 3" square, right sides together. Sew ¼" from both sides of the drawn line. Cut the unit apart on the marked line to make two half-square-triangle units. Trim the units to measure 2½" square, including seam allowances. Make four sets of four matching units.

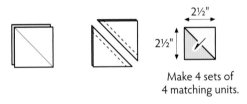

Make 4 sets of
4 matching units.

2 Lay out four matching units in two rows, rotating the units to form a pinwheel. Sew the units into rows. Join the rows to make a pinwheel unit. Make four units measuring 4½" square, including seam allowances.

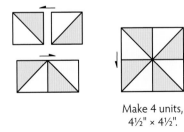

Make 4 units,
4½" × 4½".

Heart Units

1 Draw a diagonal line from corner to corner on the wrong side of the ivory 1½" squares. Layer a marked square on the upper-left corner of a dark 2½" × 4½" piece, right sides together. Sew on the marked line. Trim the excess corner fabric ¼" from the stitched line. Place a marked square on the upper-right corner of the piece. Sew and trim as before to make a unit measuring 2½" × 4½", including seam allowances. Make four pairs of matching units.

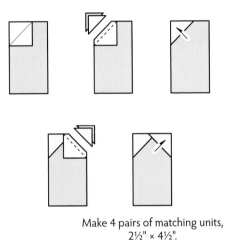

Make 4 pairs of matching units,
2½" × 4½".

2 Join two matching units from step 1 to make a unit measuring 4½" square, including seam allowances. Make four units.

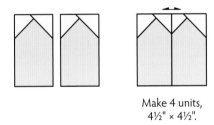

Make 4 units,
4½" × 4½".

3 Draw a diagonal line from corner to corner on the wrong side of the ivory 2½" squares. Layer a marked square on the lower-left corner of a unit from step 2. Sew on the marked line. Trim the excess corner fabric ¼" from the stitched line. Place a marked square on the lower-right corner of the

unit. Sew and trim as before to make a heart unit measuring 4½" square, including seam allowances. Make four units.

Make 4 units, 4½" × 4½".

handle with care

To make the best use of a Layer Cake square, the star-point units in the blocks are created by cutting squares in half diagonally. When assembled into units, the outside edges will be on the bias. Handle them with care while sewing and pressing so as not to distort your blocks.

MAKING THE BLOCKS

1 Join a print B triangle and an ivory triangle along their short edges. Add a contrasting A triangle, centering it on the pieced triangle. The triangles are oversized and will not match at this point. Make four matching units for star points.

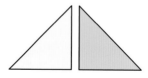 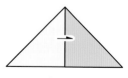

Make 4 units.

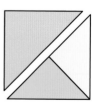

Make 4 units.

2 Align the 45° line of a square ruler with the diagonal seamline of a star-point unit as shown, making sure the 2¼" lines meet in the center of the unit and the 4½" lines on the ruler meet on the diagonal seamline. Trim along the top and right edges of the ruler.

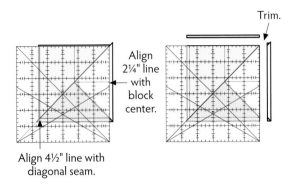

Trim.

Align 2¼" line with block center.

Align 4½" line with diagonal seam.

3 Rotate the block 180° so that you can trim the other sides. Align the 45° line of the ruler with the diagonal seamline of the block, making sure the 2¼" lines meet in the center and the 4½" lines on the ruler intersect with the previously cut edges. Trim along the top and right edges of the square ruler. Repeat the trimming steps for each of the star-point units.

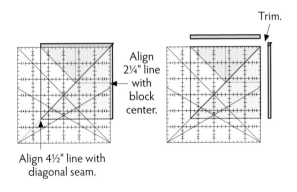

Trim.

Align 2¼" line with block center.

Align 4½" line with diagonal seam.

4 Repeat steps 1–3 to make a total of four sets of four matching star-point units measuring 4½" square, including seam allowances.

5 Lay out two rose squares, two ivory 1¾" × 3¼" pieces, two ivory 1¾" × 2" pieces, and one green print square in three rows. Sew the squares and pieces into rows. Join the rows to make a corner unit measuring 4½" square, including seam

allowances. Make 32 units. Reverse the position of the pieces in the top and bottom rows to make 32 reversed units.

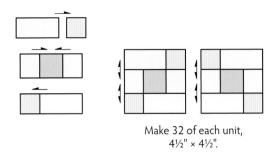

Make 32 of each unit, 4½" × 4½".

6 Lay out two corner units, two reversed corner units, four matching star-point units, and one center unit in three rows. Sew the units into rows. Join the rows to make a block measuring 12½" square, including seam allowances. Make four of each block as shown in the diagrams (16 total).

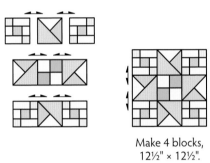

Make 4 blocks, 12½" × 12½".

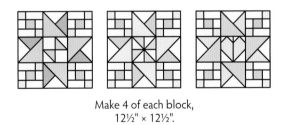

Make 4 of each block, 12½" × 12½".

make it your own!

When making the butterfly and pinwheel center units, use squares cut from a contrasting Layer Cake print instead of ivory solid for a whole new look. You can even substitute your favorite 4" finished block for more variety!

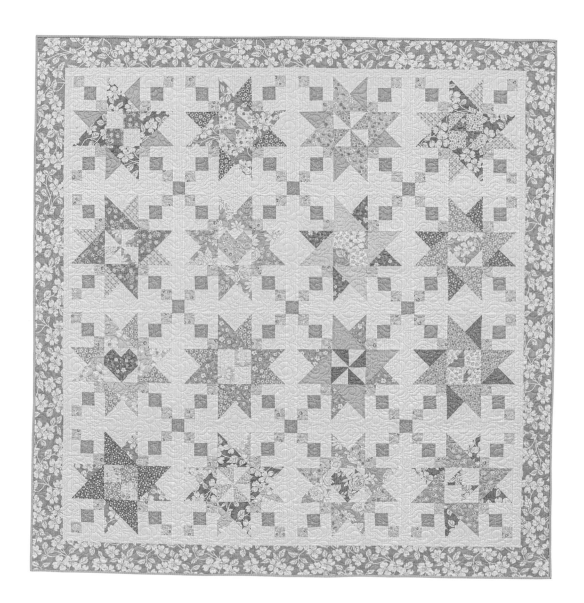

ASSEMBLING THE QUILT TOP

1 Referring to the quilt assembly diagram on page 79 for placement guidance, join four blocks and three ivory 2" × 12½" strips to make a block row. Make four rows measuring 12½" × 53", including seam allowances.

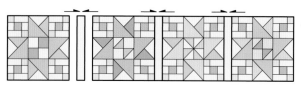

Make 4 block rows,
12½" × 53".

2 Join four ivory 2" × 12½" strips and three green print 2" squares to make a sashing row. Make three rows measuring 2" × 53", including seam allowances.

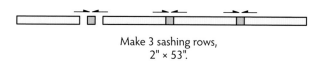

Make 3 sashing rows,
2" × 53".

3 Join the block rows and sashing rows in alternating positions as shown in the quilt assembly diagram. The quilt-top center should measure 53" square, including seam allowances.

4 Join the remaining ivory 1½"-wide strips end to end. From the pieced strip, cut two 55"-long strips and two 53"-long strips. Sew the shorter strips to opposite sides of the quilt center. Sew the longer strips to the top and bottom edges. The quilt top should measure 55" square, including seam allowances.

5 Join the green floral strips end to end. From the pieced strip, cut two 62"-long strips and two 55"-long strips. Sew the shorter strips to opposite sides of the quilt top. Sew the longer strips to the top and bottom edges to complete the quilt top. The quilt top should measure 62" square.

FINISHING THE QUILT

For more details on any finishing steps, visit ShopMartingale.com/HowtoQuilt for free downloadable information.

1 Layer the quilt top with batting and backing; baste the layers together.

2 Quilt by hand or machine. Susan's quilt was machine quilted by Sally Corona using Cascade by Keryn Emerson—an allover pattern of plumes and swirls.

3 Use the coral 2½"-wide strips to make double-fold binding. Attach the binding to the quilt.

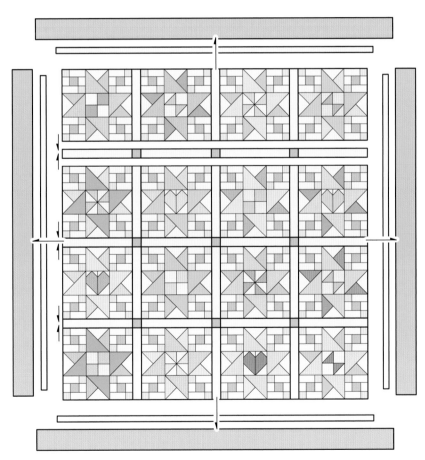

Quilt assembly

THE MODA BAKE SHOP DESIGNERS

DIANE BRINTON AND AUDREY MANN are a mother-daughter creative team. They run the Cloth Parcel, an online pattern shop and blog, where mom Diane and daughter Audrey put to use their combined decades of experience in sewing, quilting, and design. Find them online at TheClothParcel.com.

JEN DALY is a quilter and pattern designer who has been sewing all her life. She loves creating with fabrics, wool appliqué, and embroidery. Visit her at JenDalyQuilts.com and follow her on Instagram: @jendalyquilts.

JESSICA DAYON is a fabric lover, wife, and mother of four. She enjoys quilting, pattern designing, and blogging. Check out her quilt-alongs and more at JessicaDayon.blogspot.com.

NICOLA DODD has had a lifelong passion for design, and following a career in architecture, she brings the same curiosity about how things are constructed to her quilt designs. Visit Nicola at CakeStandQuilts.com or on Instagram: @cakestandquilts.

LISA JO GIRODAT is a quilter, pattern designer, knitter, mom, and grammie who loves anything to do with history. She especially enjoys watching shows about the American Revolution or Civil War. See her latest projects at NeverlandStitches.blogspot.com.

JULIE HIRT first discovered sewing and quilting in 2010 and hasn't stopped since. She offers quilting patterns, tutorials, and long-arm services. Visit her at 627Handworks.com and follow her on Instagram: @juliehirt.

SHARLA KRENZEL first began sewing at age seven and grew up to become a quilt shop owner. There she honed her quilting skills and began designing patterns. Visit Sharla at ThistleThicketStudio.com and follow her on Instagram: @thistlethicketstudio.

MICHELE KUHNS is a long-arm quilter who is busy developing her own line of patterns. The mom of two teens, she is also a Girl Scout leader. Visit Michele online at CrayonBoxQuiltStudio.com and follow her on Instagram: @crayonboxquiltstudio.

LAUREN TERRY is a pattern designer, quilter, and blogger. She began quilting while her small children were napping, and she's now hooked. Her favorite color combination for quilting is bright colors on a white background. Visit Lauren at BrightsonWhite.com.

SUSAN VAUGHAN of the Felted Pear loves to sew and quilt and also loves all things pear. Her favorite holiday is Christmas, with all the warmth and cheer and family traditions. Follow along with her sewing adventures on Instagram: @thefeltedpear.

CHRISTINE WELD lives and quilts in the Hudson Valley of New York. She laughs easily, appreciates a raucous board game night, and is a podcast aficionado. Follow her on Instagram: @christine.weld.

AMANDA WILBERT is a pattern designer who learned to quilt in 2010 with Moda precuts, and she's been hooked ever since. She began designing her own patterns in 2017. Visit Amanda at PiecedJustSew.com and follow her on Instagram: @piecedjustsew.